ZOMBIE FIGHT
BEFORE CHRISTMAS

Written by
J. Lawrence Criner

Illustrated by
Robert W. Cabell

Edited by
Robert W. Cabell

Published by

Warrington Press
Renton Washington & Brooklyn New York

2016 All rights reserved.
ISBN: 978-0-9984331-0-3 (paperback)

Printed in the United States of America

Dedicated to

Alfred Lord Noyes
who inspired my first poetic pursuits

'Twas the night
before Christmas
and all through the cave
The reindeer were rising
undead from their grave

The soil was
sifted through the bones
of their ribs while
serial Santa dreamed of
children in cribs.

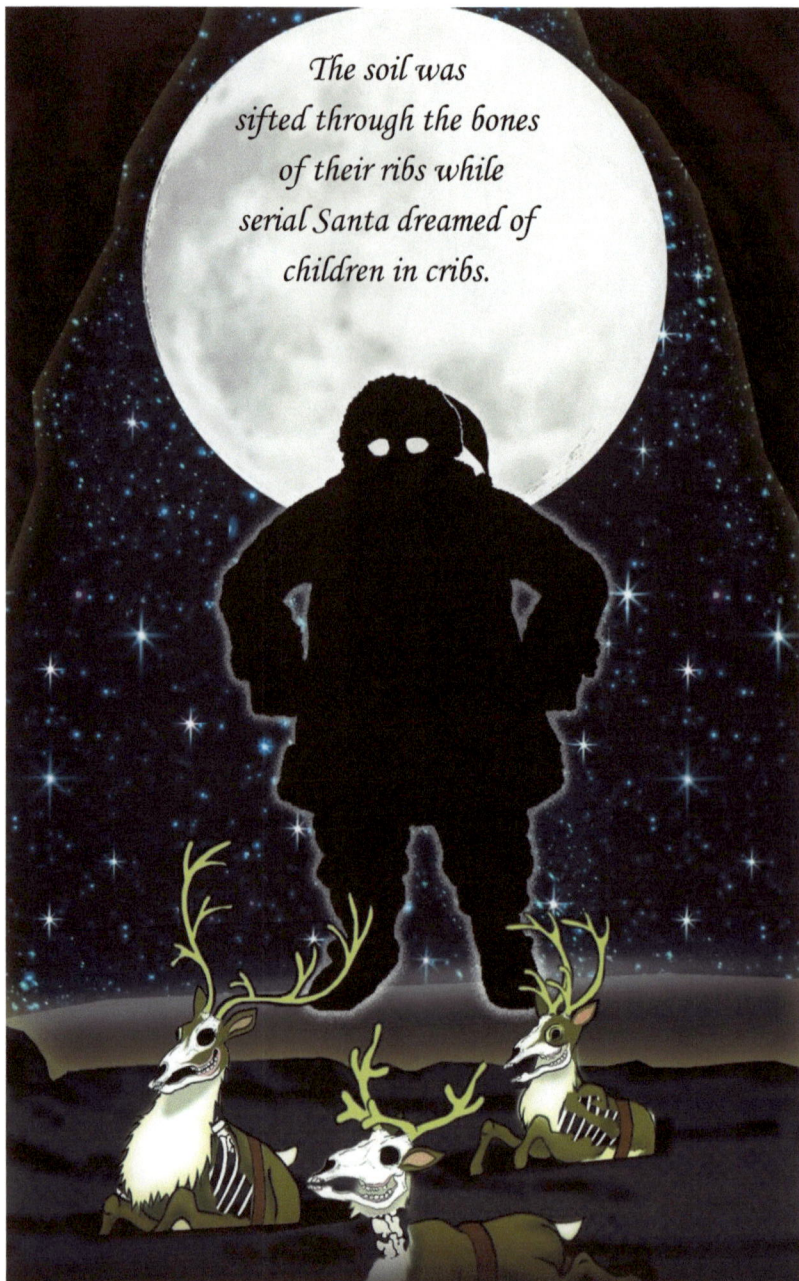

Each child was nestled in
their own Kevlar vest
While visions of feeding
deprived them of rest.
As mother field stripped
her AK-47.
Father oiled the action
of his 1911.

"The time we have's fleeting,"
Santa anxiously cried
As reindeer shook beetles
from the holes in their hide.
"Up, Biter!
Up, Clencher!
Up, Razor
and Ripper!
Up, Hellborn!
Up, Onyx and
Arterial Sipper!"

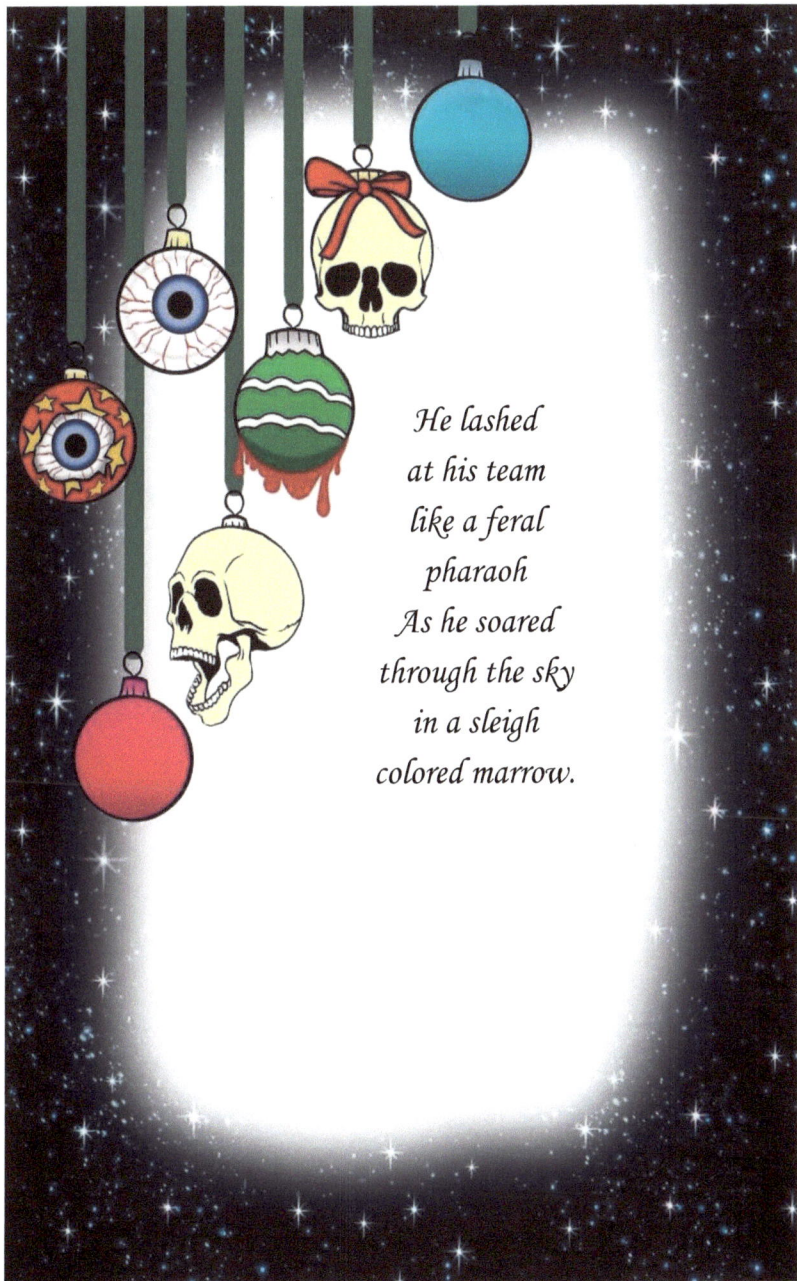

He lashed
at his team
like a feral
pharaoh
As he soared
through the sky
in a sleigh
colored marrow.

He circled, surveilling
until he found a nice spot
Then he dove like a fighter
that was coming in hot.

Soon out on the lawn
there came quite a racket
Mother grabbed rifle,
threw on her flak jacket.
But father was sleepy,
caught off guard by the sound
As the runners of sleigh
impacted hard ground.

The figure that bounded
from the sleigh was a fright
That stilled human hearts
on this cold winter night.

Fur-trimmed
and ferocious
standing next
to his team
Whose hooves
were like razors
with whetted-edge gleam.
He wore a long beard
like a Hollywood druid
Though splattered with plasma
and post-mortem fluid.
Filthy fabric of clothing
absorbed every drop.
He resembled a butcher
just come from his shop.

With his eyes
red from malice
that shined in the night
And hungry lips eager
for his midnight delight,
This red suited figure
appeared quite a fellow —
A malevolent mass
of murderous Jell-O

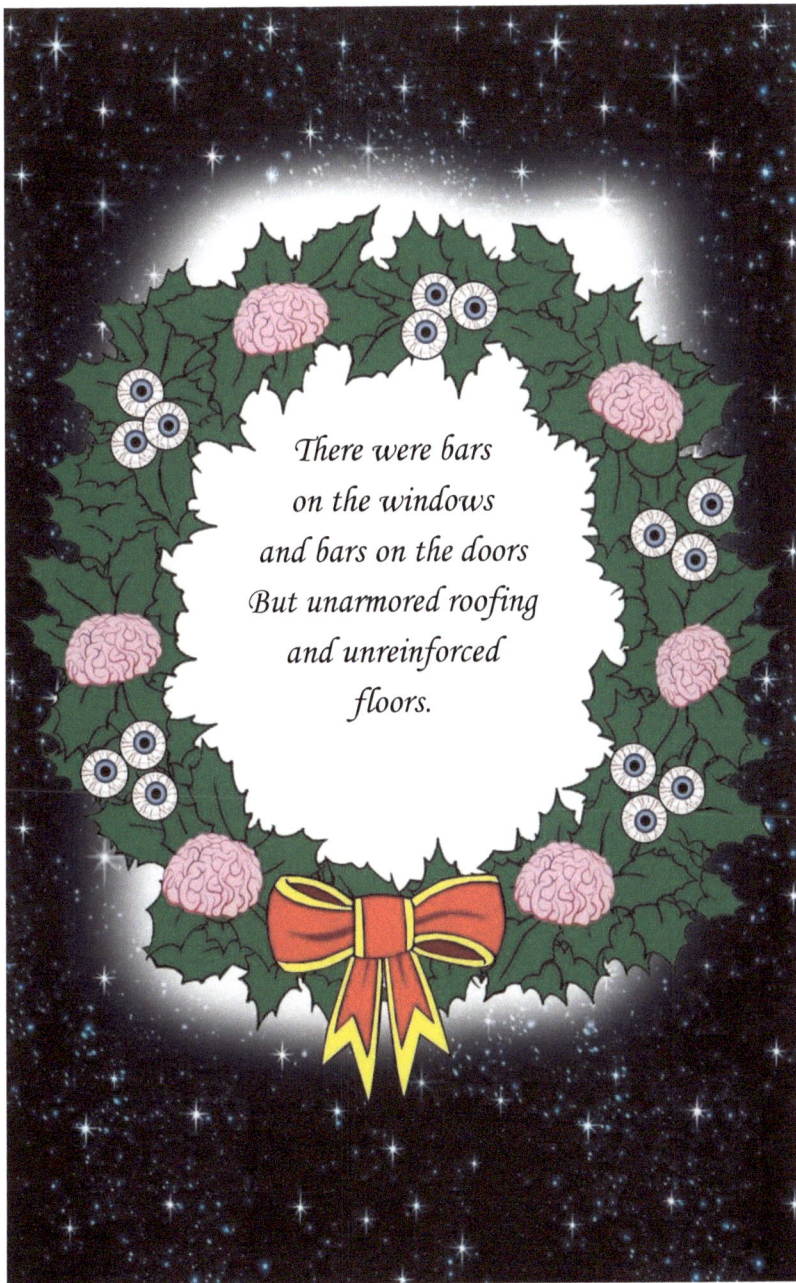

There were bars
on the windows
and bars on the doors
But unarmored roofing
and unreinforced
floors.

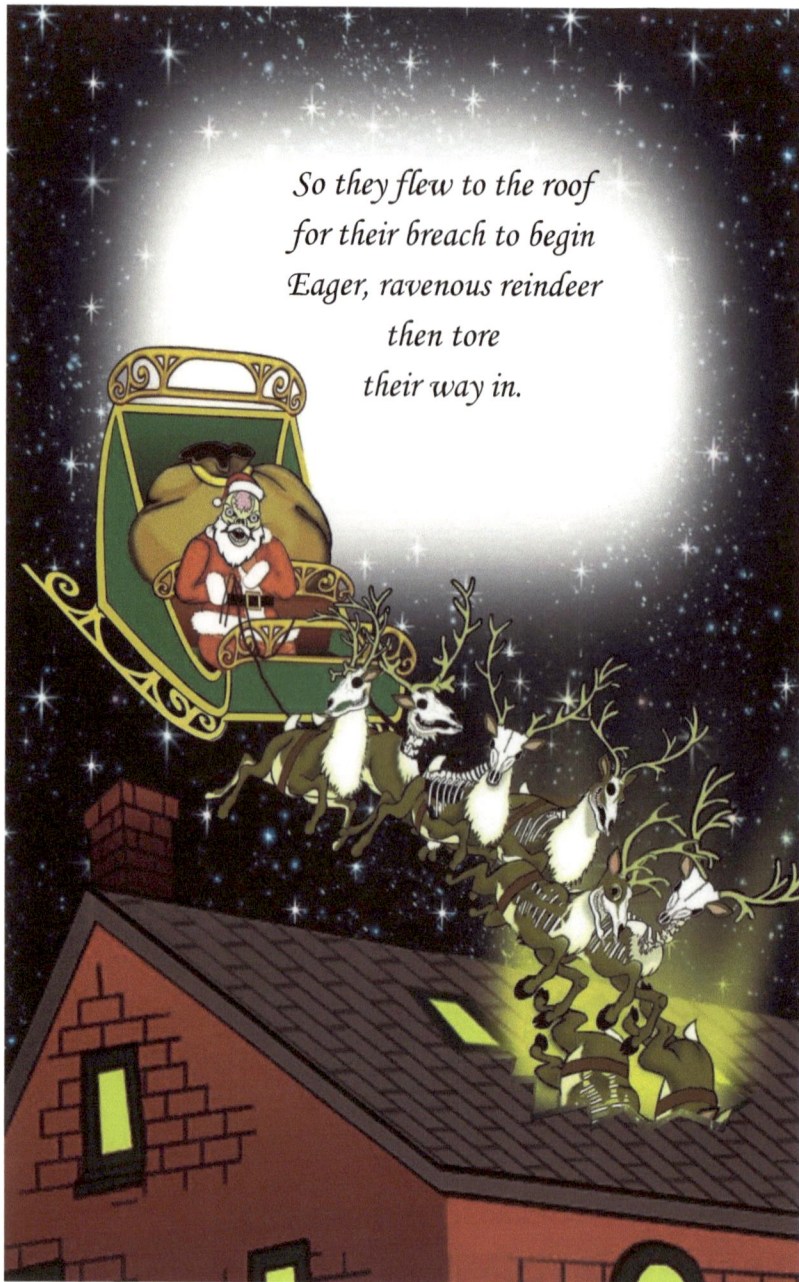

So they flew to the roof
for their breach to begin
Eager, ravenous reindeer
then tore
their way in.

Soon the powder of plaster
was falling like snow
On holiday morsels
that were laid out below.
There were sweetmeats
and fruitcakes
and tangerines whole
Spread out on the table
near crystal punchbowl.

But Santa was seeking
a meal much more filling
And sought to fill sleigh bed
with flesh from his killing.
He'd begin with the children
and move on from there
'Til he'd shed every drop
and plucked every hair.

Then Santa and reindeer
both raced down the stair
All hungry for humans
though refusing to share.
The screams of
the household
were joy to his ears
As he feasted on family
and drank up their tears.

There was blood on the baseboard,
blood on the wall.
There was blood on the carpet
where the children's feet fall.
There was blood on the floorboards,
blood on the ceiling
From carnage he caused
he found crimson appealing.

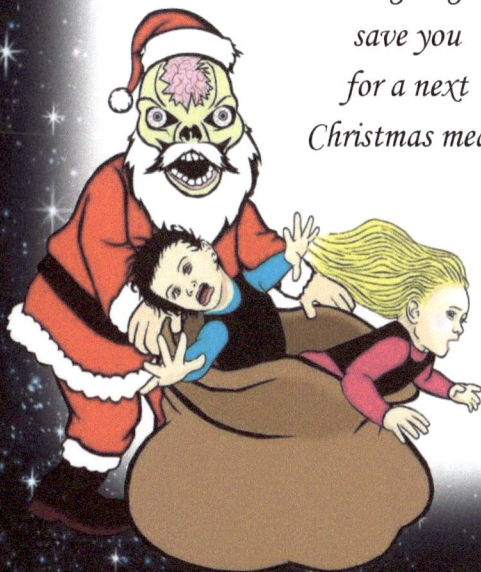

Though Santa was savage
he also was kind
By killing only
the victims he'd find.
If you could escape him
and you could conceal,
He'd begrudgingly
save you
for a next
Christmas meal.

But Santa was saddened
at the stains on the floor
As thirst was unsated
and he hungered for more
So he went house to house
and he went block by block
Then he gave earth a year
to replenish his stock.

The End

About The Author

J. Lawrence Criner's credits include travel journalism, technical writing, classic poetry. Mr. Criner is an avid student of the Gaelic culture and epic poems. He lives in the Seattle area, where diversity is celebrated and has now focused his varied talents on creating classic Zombie literature.